The Things Birds Eat

Betsey Chessen

Scholastic Inc.

New York - Toronto - London - Auckland - Sydney

Acknowledgments

Science Consultants: Patrick R. Thomas, Ph.D., Bronx Zoo/Wildlife Conservation Park;
Glenn Phillips, The New York Botanical Garden
Literacy Specialist: Ada Cordova, District 2, New York City

Design: MKR Design, Inc.

Photo Research: Barbara Scott

Endnotes: Samantha Berger

Endnote Illustrations: Craig Spearing

———————————————

Photographs: Cover: Martin Harvey/The Wildlife Collection; p. 1: Joe McDonald/DRK Photo;
p. 2: Alan D. Carey/Photo Researhers; p. 3:Johann Schumacher/Peter Arnold; p. 4: Helen
Williams/Photo Researchers; p. 5: Richard R. Hansen/Photo Researchers; p. 6: Joe McDonald/DRK
Photo; p. 7: Gregory K. Scott/Photo Researchers; p. 8: Wyman Meinzer/Peter Arnold; p. 9: Gunter
Zeisler /Peter Arnold; p. 10: Manfred Daneggar/Peter Arnold; p. 11: S. Nielsen/DRK Photo;
p. 12: Mark A. Chappell/Animals, Animals.

Library of Congress Cataloging-in-Publication Data
Chessen, Betsey 1970-
The things birds eat! / Betsey Chessen.
p. cm. -- (Science emergent readers)
Includes index.
Summary: Simple text and photographs present birds eating a
variety of things, including worms, seeds, and fish.
ISBN 0-590-76965-0 (pbk.: alk. paper)
1. Birds--Food--Juvenile literature. [1. Birds--Food.]
I. Title.   II. Series.
QL698.4.C48   1998

598. 15'3--dc21

98-18824
CIP AC

1   2   3   4   5   6   7   8   9   10   08   03   02   01   00   99   98

Birds eat many things.

Fly catcher

Birds eat worms. Robin

Birds eat caterpillars.

Warbler

Birds eat seeds.

Birds eat sap.

sapsucker

Birds eat nectar.

Birds eat berries.

Cedar Waxwing

Birds eat lizards.

Roadrunner

Birds eat frogs.

ground hornbill

Birds eat mice. Kestrel

Birds eat fish.

Great Blue Heron

Birds even eat starfish!

Gull

Things Birds Eat

Different birds eat different things, but all birds eat! Birds find food by catching insects, fishing, grazing, searching for seeds, and hunting. Here are some examples of different kinds of birds and the different things they eat.

Can you guess how the flycatcher (page 1) got its name? There are about 300 different species of flycatcher in the world, and they have incredible aim. Flycatchers are well known for catching flies, butterflies, and dragonflies in mid-air!

Robins (page 2) feed mostly on ground dwellers like caterpillars, spiders, and worms. A robin can actually feel the movement of an earthworm underground, turn over the dirt, find the worm there, and feast. On a good day, a robin will eat about 14 worms!

Warblers (pages 2–3) feed on insects and arthropods, but at the end of the summer they supplement their diet with berries and fruit.

Cardinals (page 4) eat weeds, seeds, berries, insects, and larvae. Their small strong beaks are particularly well suited to picking up smaller food items and breaking open seeds.

The sapsucker (page 5) is a member of the woodpecker family. It drills holes into trees and sucks out sap and insects from inside. Some types of woodpecker can extend their tongue inches beyond the tip of their beak to get food hidden deep within the wood!

Hummingbirds (page 6) live on nectar and bugs. They consume their own weight in nectar every day. Hummingbirds and flowers help each other to survive. The flowers give the hummingbirds nectar to eat.

Hummingbirds help pollinate the flower. This kind of relationship, in which two things help each other, is called symbiosis.

The cedar waxwing (page 6-7) is very fond of fruit. These birds are often found perched in rows, passing a berry from one to the next to the next. They like fruit so much, they will often descend upon an orchard, devour all the fruit, and disappear. Some have been known to eat fruit until they can barely fly.

The roadrunner (page 8) eats mostly snakes (even poisonous ones!). It also eats grasshoppers, birds, mice, and lizards. A roadrunner will catch its prey and batter it repeatedly on the ground, to injure or stun it, then swallow it head-first.

The ground hornbill (page 9) seeks out big fruit-bearing trees. It lives mostly on fruit but also eats snakes, grasshoppers, and lizards. The edges of its bill are serrated so that food can be tightly gripped. The bird tosses its food in the air and then catches and swallows it.

Kestrels (page 10) are one of the best known and most abundant birds of prey. They eat ducks, birds, mice, and chickens, often in mid-air!

Great blue herons (page 10–11) feed on aquatic creatures such as fish, frogs, and tadpoles, but also on adult insects, larvae, small mammals, worms, and crustaceans.

Gulls (page 12) eat almost anything that meets their eye, edible or not. They have a reputation for being thieves. They steal food from picnics or garbage from the trash can and fly away. They also eat live and dead fish, rodents, birds, insects, plants, and most anything else. Gulls are clever birds and will often drop shellfish from great heights, in order to break the shell, and eat the flesh within.